United States Marine Corps

BRUNO LURCH

Heinemann Library
Chicago, Illinois

Series design by Heinemann Library
Page layout by Malcolm Walker
Photo research by Bill Broyles
Printed and bound in China by
  WKT Company Limited.

08 07 06 05 04
10 9 8 7 6 5 4 3 2 1

Library of Congress Cataloging-in-Publication Data

Lurch, Bruno, 1956-
  United States Marine Corps / Bruno Lurch.
     p. cm. -- (U.S. Armed Forces)
Includes bibliographical references and index.
  ISBN 1-4034-4551-6 (hardcover) -- ISBN 1-4034-4557-5
(pbk.)
  1. United States. Marine Corps--Juvenile literature. [1.
United
States. Marine Corps.] I. Title. II. U.S. Armed Forces
(Series)
  VE23.L87 2004
  359.9'6'0973--dc22
                    2003023785

Produced for Heinemann Library by
White-Thomson Publishing Ltd
2/3 St Andrew's Place
Lewes UK   BN7 1UP

Acknowledgments
The author and publisher are grateful to the following for permission
to reproduce copyright material:
Title page, Faleh Kheiber/Reuters/Corbis; contents page, Military
Stock Photography;
p. 4 U.S. Marine Corps; p. 5 Defense Visual Information Center; p.
6 U.S. Marine Corps; p. 7t Defense Visual Information Center; p.7b
U.S. Navy; pp. 8, 9, 10, 11 U.S. Marine Corps; p. 12 National
Archives and Records Administration; p. 13 U.S. Marine Corps; p.
14 National Archives and Records Administration; p 15t,
Bettmann/Corbis; p. 15b Faleh Kheiber/Reuters/Corbis; pp. 16, 17
U.S. Marine Corps; p. 18 Defense Visual Information Center; p. 19
U.S. Marine Corps; pp. 20, 21 Defense Visual Information Center;
pp. 22, 23 U.S. Marine Corps; pp. 24, 25 U.S. Navy; p. 26 Defense
Visual Information Center; p. 27 U.S. Marine Corps; p. 28, Military
Stock Photography; pp. 29, 30 Defense Visual Information Center;
pp. 31, 32, 33, 34, 35 U.S. Marine Corps; p. 36 Bettmann/Corbis;
p. 37 U.S. Marine Corps; pp. 38, 39 Medal of Honor Society; pp.
40, 41, National Archives and Records Administration; p 41b
Defense Visual Information Center; pp. 42, 43 U.S. Marine Corps;
pp. 44, 45 U.S. Marine Band Library.
Cover photograph by David Turnley/Corbis
Every effort has been made to contact copyright holders of
any material reproduced in this book. Any omissions will be
rectified in subsequent printings if notice is given to the
publisher.

Special thanks to Lt. Col G.A. Lofaro for his review of
this book.

Note to the Reader: Some words are shown in
bold, **like this.** You can find out what they
mean by looking in the glossary.

Contents

What Is the Marine Corps?

The United States Marine Corps is one of the branches of the armed forces of the United States. The other branches are the army, the navy, the air force, and the Coast Guard. The Marine Corps is part of the United States Department of the Navy. However, the marines have their own set of rules. Marines also wear different uniforms.

The word *marine* means "of or related to the sea." However, the marines are trained to fight at sea, on land, and in the air. They train to fight in all kinds of climates. The marines have fought in Mexico, North Africa, Korea, Europe, the Pacific islands, and Iraq.

The Commandant

The person in charge of the Marine Corps is a four-star general. The general's title is Commandant of the United States Marine Corps. He reports to the secretary of the navy, who is appointed by the president.

A marine carries a "wounded" teammate during a jungle evacuation training exercise.

4

These U.S. Marines are crisply saluting at Camp Lejeune, North Carolina.

The United States Marine Corps motto is *Semper fidelis*, or *Semper fi*, Latin for "always faithful." These words tell how the marines feel about their country and about one another.

The work of the marines

The Marine Corps helps to defend the nation on both land and sea. The corps is always ready to do this.

The **combat units** of the Marine Corps include three **Marine Expeditionary Forces.** One is in the Atlantic Ocean and two are in the Pacific Ocean. These forces are ready to fight at all times. Some units of marines help the U.S. Navy by defending naval stations in the United States and other parts of the world. Some marines serve on navy warships. On U.S. shores, the marines watch over **navy yards.**

The marines work during times of peace as well as times of war. For example, marines are stationed at American **embassies** in other countries. There, they guard property and protect lives. In the United States, **units** of marines sometimes help communities that have been damaged by floods, hurricanes, and other disasters.

The Marine Corps guards the White House. It also performs other jobs that the president gives out. The United States Marine Corps Band gives public performances and plays at presidential functions.

Qualities of a marine

Marines are expected to be honest and brave. They must obey the law and lead by example. They must also respect themselves and others. The marines are expected to support and defend the United States Constitution. Marines must fulfill their duties and behave correctly at all times. If their behavior is bad, they must accept their punishment.

A U.S. Marine stands guard at the U.S. embassy in Kabul, Afghanistan.

A marine reserve unit falls back during a training exercise in California.

The Marine Corps Reserve

The Marine Corps Reserve is the backup force of the Marine Corps. The reserves have trained people ready for **active duty** in case of war or a national emergency. People in the Marine Corps Reserves are not full-time marines. They train one weekend each month and two weeks during the summer. Reserve units take part in more than twenty training drills each year.

In the 2000s, more than 100,000 reserve marines were assigned to 289 reserve **units** at 185 locations in the United States.

Toys for Tots

During the 1947 Christmas season, Bill Hendricks, a Marine Corps Reserve major, gathered and handed out 5,000 toys to poor children in the Los Angeles area. The Marine Corps continued the program the following year. Only this time, toys were handed out nationwide—and the Marine Corps Reserve Toys for Tots program was born. Each year, around seven million toys are handed out.

A marine sergeant plays catch with children at an Italian orphanage after handing out Christmas toys.

The Founding of the Marines

The **Continental Congress** started the Marine Corps on November 10, 1775, to fight in the Revolutionary War (1775–1783). The marines were called the Continental Marines. They consisted of two **battalions.**

The Continental Marines fought on land and at sea during the Revolutionary War. Their first battle was in February 1776. They fought the British on the Delaware River near Philadelphia. They made their first amphibious attack in March 1776 in the Bahamas. This took place under the command of Captain (later Major) Samuel Nicholas.

Know It

November 10th is celebrated each year as the birthday of the United States Marine Corps.

First Commissioned Officer

Captain Samuel Nicholas was the Marines' first commissioned officer. Nicholas was the highest-ranking marine during the Revolutionary War. He is thought to be the first United States Marine Commandant.

The Treaty of Paris in April 1783 ended the Revolutionary War. When the last of the navy's ships were sold, the Continental navy and marines were no longer in service.

Congress sets up the Marine Corps

Then on July 11, 1798, the United States Congress passed a law that set up the Marine Corps again. Its main job was to protect American ships from attacks by pirate ships and by British navy ships. In the late 1700s, the marines also fought some naval battles against France. At this time, the marines were mainly located on board ships. They were expert shooters who were in charge of the **gun turrets.**

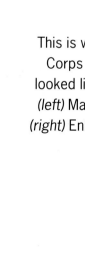

This is what Marine Corps members looked like in 1798. *(left)* Marine Officer *(right)* Enlisted Marine

Marines in the 1800s

During the 1800s, the marines fought bravely in all United States wars. Between 1801 and 1805, the United States fought pirates, called the Barbary pirates, in the Mediterranean Sea. The Barbary pirates attacked the ships of several nations, including the United States. In 1805, the marines stormed the headquarters of the Barbary pirates in Derna, Tripoli (now a part of the North African country of Libya). Their victory helped to end the pirate raids.

A Sword as Thanks

First Lieutenant Presley Neville O'Bannon raised the American flag over the captured headquarters of the Barbary pirates. He became the first marine officer to raise the American flag outside the United States. One story says that a thankful North African desert chieftain gave O'Bannon a jeweled sword. It was a gift from the Mamelukes, fierce desert warriors of North Africa. Such swords had become a part of the gear worn by all marine officers by 1825. Marine officers still wear them today.

Marines fight at Quantanamo in Cuba during the Spanish-American War (1898). Quantanamo is still an American base.

Marine actions in 1800s wars

In the War of 1812 (1812–1815) against the British, the marines helped the United States win the sea battles. In the Civil War (1861–1865), small numbers of marines fought in several land and naval battles. Their main job was to guard ships and forts. In the Spanish-American War in 1898, the marines were the first American troops to land in Cuba. The war was partly fought to help Cuba become free of Spanish rule.

"Eighth and Eye"

The oldest Marine Corps post is located in southeast Washington, D.C. It is nicknamed "Eighth and Eye," because it is located between Eighth and Ninth Streets and G and I Streets. President Thomas Jefferson selected this location in 1801. Today, it is home to the United States Marine Corps Band.

Marines in World War I and World War II

The marines played an important part in winning World War I (1914–1918). Marine **sharpshooters** fought bravely against the Germans in several places in France. Marine pilots flew bombing missions. About 30,000 marines served in France during World War I. More than 10,000 were killed or wounded in the fighting.

Battle of Belleau Wood

The marines fought fiercely against the Germans in the Battle of Belleau Wood, a forest located outside Paris, France. The marines succeeded in pushing the Germans out of the forest. The French people were so grateful to the marines that they nicknamed Belleau Wood the Forest of the Marine Brigade.

Thousands of marines fought bravely during World War II (1939–1945). They played an important part in many battles against Japan on the islands in the Pacific Ocean. In August 1942, the marines invaded Guadalcanal in the Solomon Islands. They continued to defeat the Japanese on other islands in the Pacific. At one point, more than 450,000 marines were involved in fighting World War II. Nearly 87,000 died or were wounded. Eighty-two marines earned the Medal of Honor for their bravery in the war.

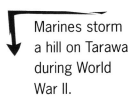

Marines storm a hill on Tarawa during World War II.

Anthony Casamento's Bravery

Corporal Anthony Casamento was the leader of a machine-gun squad during the battle on Guadalcanal. One night his squad came under heavy enemy fire. All 29 members of his squad were killed or wounded. Although Casamento was seriously wounded, he continued to shoot at the enemy. This helped protect other groups of marines. Casamento was then sent to a military hospital in California.

In 1964, it was learned that two eyewitnesses to Casamento's bravery were still alive. Their stories set in motion the chain of events that ended with President Jimmy Carter awarding Casamento a Medal of Honor in 1980—38 years after his bravery in Guadalcanal.

Navajo Code Talkers

The Marine Corps Navajo Code Talkers was a program set up during World War II. In this program, the marines used Navajo as a code language when sending radio and telegraph messages. Only the Navajo people could understand it. Using this language kept the enemy from intercepting the messages.

Two Navajo code talkers use a radio to send a message in their native language.

Marines in Korea, Vietnam, and the Gulf Wars

Marines fought during the Korean War between 1950 and 1953. The war was between the Asian countries of North Korea and South Korea. The war started when troops from **communist** North Korea invaded South Korea. More than 25,000 marines were killed or wounded during the Korean War. In addition to their **combat** duties, the marines served in helicopters, which were called transport choppers during the war. Marine helicopters moved troops and cargo to battle zones. They also moved the wounded. Marine helicopters brought out more than 10,000 wounded soldiers. Many soldiers survived their injuries because they were brought out so quickly.

A marine helicopter brings in troops to relieve a South Korean **unit** in 1951.

In Vietnam

About 450,000 marines fought in the Vietnam War between 1965 and 1971. This was the longest war the marines had ever fought in. The Vietnam War involved two countries—North Vietnam and South Vietnam. It started when communist forces in North Vietnam tried to end the government of South Vietnam. North Vietnamese forces also wanted to join the two countries into one country. The marines, the army, and other U.S. armed forces fought on the side of South Vietnam. More than 13,000 marines were killed, and more than 88,000 were wounded in the Vietnam War.

These Marines are on a **reconnaissance** mission in Vietnam.

In the Persian Gulf

In 1990, the country of Iraq invaded the small country of Kuwait, located in southwest Asia. Both of these countries are on a body of water called the Persian Gulf. The United States, together with other countries, fought Iraq to force it to leave Kuwait. More than 92,000 marines were involved in this Gulf War. It was the greatest use of Marine Corps troops since the Vietnam War. Twenty-four marines were killed in the war, and 92 were wounded. In 2003, the United States was once again involved in a war against Iraq. Again, the marines were involved in both combat and other kinds of duties.

U.S. Marines stand guard as an Iraqi policeman runs to arrest men in a house after a demonstration in July 2003.

15

Basic Training

Before the early 1800s, there was no program for training Marine Corps **recruits.** New marines were taught only military drills and how to use a rifle.

However, Franklin Wharton understood the importance of a good training program. He was commandant from 1804 to 1818. Wharton organized a school for marine recruits in Washington, D.C. He made sure that all marines carried the same military equipment and wore the same uniform.

These are marines who served during the Civil War.

Enlistment Oath

An individual who enlists in the Marine Corps—and all the armed forces—makes the following oath: "I do solemnly swear that I will support and defend the Constitution of the United States against all enemies, foreign and domestic. That I will bear true faith and allegiance to the same; and that I will obey the orders of the President of the United States and the orders of the officers appointed over me, according to regulations and the Uniform Code of Military Justice. So help me God."

First training program

In 1911, William P. Biddle became the Marine Corps commandant. He wanted all marines to be trained and prepared for **combat** at any time.

One of Biddle's first actions was to require several months of training for every Marine Corps recruit. He set up four training centers. They were located in Pennsylvania, Virginia, Washington State, and California. He planned a training course that included physical fitness, drills, hand-to-hand combat, and rifle **marksmanship.**

The basic training a marine receives has changed little since 1911. Only during World War II was the training time reduced to four weeks. The result, however, was a poorly trained fighting force. The Marine Corps has since decided that seven to eight weeks is the minimum time required for recruit training.

Major General William P. Biddle (1853–1923) served in the Marine Corps for 38 years. He is buried in Arlington National Cemetery.

Recruits march on the parade deck at Parris Island, South Carolina.

Basic training today

Today, marine **recruits** who live east of the Mississippi River are sent to Parris Island, South Carolina, to complete their basic training course. Those who live west of the Mississippi train in San Diego, California. Advanced training at Camp Lejeune, North Carolina, or Camp Pendleton, California, follows basic training.

All marine recruits first spend three to five days in Receiving. Here they get their uniforms, learn to march, and get used to following orders. They also take the Initial Strength Test (IST). Men must be able to do 2 dead-hang pull-ups, 44 crunches (a kind of sit-up) in 2 minutes, and run 1.5 miles (2.5 kilometers) in 13.5 minutes. Women must be able to do a flex-arm (bent-arm) hang for 12 seconds and 44 crunches in 2 minutes, and run 1.5 miles in 15 minutes.

Any recruit who does not pass the IST must go to the Physical Conditioning **Platoon** for at least 21 days (17 days for women). Male recruits do not get out until they can do 3 pull-ups and 50 sit-ups in 2 minutes, and run 3 miles (4.8 kilometers) in 28 minutes.

Know It

There is no military academy for young people hoping to become marine officers. Usually, those who want to become marine officers enroll at the U.S. Naval Academy in Annapolis, Maryland.

At boot camp

Marine **boot camp** lasts thirteen weeks. Recruits wake up each morning at 5:30 A.M. and train daily for sixteen hours. Each training group is assigned three drill instructors, called DIs. The DIs are marines who teach recruits important military behavior, duties, and **combat** skills.

While in training, recruits get into good physical shape. They must march as far as 10 miles (16 kilometers) carrying a heavy backpack and do stretches, sit-ups, pull-ups, and push-ups nearly every day. They learn how to shoot a rifle, patrol, and set up camp. They learn about first aid and get trained in martial arts. They learn how to operate equipment. They also spend time in the classroom, where subjects include military history.

Recruits yell "Aye, aye, sir!" as a drill instructor directs them back to their quarters.

The Crucible

The final test a recruit faces before completing boot camp is called the Crucible. It is a demanding 54-hour exercise in which recruits are sent out into the field. There they perform difficult mental and physical exercises. The aim of the Crucible is to show the recruits how important it is for marines to work as a team. During the Crucible, recruits are required to use all the skills they have learned in boot camp.

Jobs for Marines

The main job of a marine is to be a skilled fighter. Marines are often involved in **combat** with the enemy. So they have to be good at fighting, using weapons, and operating different kinds of machinery.

Combat jobs

Many marines are foot soldiers. They are assigned to the **infantry**. The infantry is most likely to come in direct contact with the enemy. Jobs in the infantry include being a member of a **light-armored vehicle** crew, being a machine gunner or missile operator, or working in **reconnaissance.**

Noncombat jobs

Not all marines have jobs that put them in direct contact with the enemy. Some work in jobs known as combat support. These marines help the infantry as a crew member of a tank or **amphibious assault vehicle.**

Marines operate a tank in the field. Note the driver is peering out from under the gun.

A helicopter pilot prepares for a flight by making his flight check before takeoff.

Marines fly airplanes and helicopters. In addition to the pilot and copilot, a typical aircraft flight crew includes a crew chief and a **navigator.**

Some marines work closely with infantry members. They help them as **radar** operators or by predicting weather conditions and putting out fires. Others work on airplane and helicopter support crews. These marines direct pilots when to take off and land and make sure that aircraft and equipment are in top shape.

The Marine Corps Association is the professional association for all marines. They can be on **active duty,** in the reserves, or **retired.** It was started in 1913. Its purpose is to share information about the Marine Corps and to keep up its spirit and traditions. To do this, the association publishes two magazines, the *Marine Corps Gazette* and *Leatherneck.*

A marine computer repair technician fixes a computer.

Marines also are **communications** technicians. They create computer programs and graphics and operate and repair **state-of-the-art** computers.

Scholarships

The Marine Corps Scholarship Foundation provides college **scholarships** for children of marines, especially those who were killed or wounded in action. During the 2002–2003 school year, 848 students received more than $1 million in financial aid from the foundation. Individuals, foundations, small businesses, and large corporations donate money for the scholarships. Formal dances, golf tournaments, and other events also raise money.

Marines also work as military police officers. They keep order on bases and arrest those marines who break the law. Some marines are lawyers who prosecute or defend marines accused of breaking the law.

A marine dog in training runs an obstacle course to learn how to catch a suspect.

Marine Dogs

Not all jobs in the Marine Corps are held by humans. During World War II (1939–1945), the Corps began using with dogs in **combat.** Starting in 1942, dogs were trained to deliver messages from battlefronts to headquarters and scout battle sites. Individual dog owners donated their dogs. The Doberman Pinscher Club of America and Dogs for Defense also provided dogs. The Marine Corps also used Airedale terriers and German and Belgian shepherds. Each animal had to be between one and five years old, weigh at least 50 pounds (23 kilograms), and stand at least 25 inches (62.5 centimeters) tall. The dogs were trained for fourteen weeks.

A Marine's Weapons and Equipment

Aircraft

Marines in **combat** have **state-of-the-art** weapons and equipment. Some operate **fixed-wing aircraft.** This kind of aircraft is used to attack and destroy targets on land and protect ground forces. It is also used to fight enemy aircraft, fly **reconnaissance** missions, and refuel other aircraft while in the air.

Some marines operate helicopters, or **rotary-wing aircraft.** This kind of aircraft is used to attack the enemy and transport supplies and equipment.

A fixed-wing AV-8B Harrier makes a vertical landing aboard an **amphibious assault** ship after operations in southern Iraq.

Aircraft Costs

Advanced weapons are expensive. The AV-8B Harrier II aircraft, which attacks and destroys targets on land, costs about $28 million. The EA-6B Prowler, which attacks targets and protects ground forces, is even more costly at $52 million. An AH-1W Super Cobra attack helicopter costs more than $10 million. A CH-53E Super Stallion helicopter, which carries supplies and equipment, is priced at just over $26 million.

A rotary-wing CH-53E Super Stallion takes off from an amphibious assault ship during Operation Iraqi Freedom.

An amphibious assault vehicle launches from a ship's well deck during a mock landing exercise.

Weapons

The M136 AT4 antitank weapon weighs less than 15 pounds (almost 7 kilograms). That's only as heavy as a large bag of dog food or kitty litter. But it can still destroy an enemy tank. The Shoulder-Launched Multipurpose Assault Weapon does not weigh much more. It can destroy tanks and bunkers where enemy soldiers may be hiding.

The Dragon Weapon System can weigh as much as 48 pounds (almost 22 kilograms) and has a great deal of firepower. The Dragon allows a single marine to destroy armored vehicles without any help. One model is designed for night combat, while another is used during the day. Other Marine Corps weaponry includes light and medium howitzers (cannons), machine and submachine guns, shotguns, rifles, pistols, mortars, and grenade launchers.

The M1A1, the basic marine battle tank, can attack the enemy on land or in water. Amphibious Assault Vehicles are tanks that are specially designed for operating in water or on land. Laser equipment is used to locate targets and steer laser-guided rockets or missiles to their targets. The Stinger Weapons System is a portable, easy-to-move-around, guided missile system. It allows marines to defend against air attacks at low altitudes.

Birds of Prey?

Marines use Shrike and Sparrow missiles, which target enemy aircraft, anti-aircraft **radar**, and tanks. The Hawk Surface-to-Air Missile System provides defense against enemy missiles.

Equipment

Combat Rubber **Reconnaissance** Craft are small, inflatable boats. They are used on reconnaissance missions. On missions that start in the air, marines use Parachute Individual Equipment Kits. These contain jumpsuits, jumpsuit liners, gloves, boots, and helmets.

Radios send out voice messages and **data** from land-to-land or air-to-land. Meteorological Measuring Sets obtain information about weather conditions. Firefinders are movable **radar units** that detect enemy **artillery** and **mortar** fire. Mine detectors locate and remove the fuses from land mines. Underwater Breathing Apparatus Systems allow divers to remain underwater for four hours. Water Purification Units clean contaminated water.

Infrared Aiming Lights give off light that cannot be seen by the naked eye. While operating these lights, marines wear Night Vision Goggles and use Weapon Night Sights to find the enemy and aim and fire weapons.

A marine fills a water bladder with water from the Reverse Osmosis Water Purification Unit.

Marines wear protective clothing after an alarm sounds at their camp in Kuwait in February 2003

Biological or Chemical Warfare Clothing

Some clothing is designed to protect marines during biological or chemical warfare. One outfit includes a full-length zippered coat with a hood and a protective flap. The pants can be adjusted at the waist and closed tight at the bottom of each leg. Special shoes protect the feet from chemicals, and protective masks guard the face, eyes, and **respiratory system.** These masks do not prevent the marines from seeing, speaking, or hearing. They can be worn for up to twelve hours.

Special clothing

Marines have specially designed clothing that protects them. One outfit includes a parka with six pockets and a hood and pants with suspenders, belt loops, two pockets, and zippers that run to the knees. The zippers make the pants easy to put on and take off while wearing boots. The clothes are windproof and waterproof.

Other outfits allow the marines to keep warm in very cold temperatures. The Intermediate Cold Wet Boot, made of leather with a waterproof liner, protects the marines from wet or cold weather.

Emblems, Battle Colors, and Flags

Emblems, battle colors, and flags are a basic part of Marine Corps tradition. The Eagle, Globe, and Anchor emblem is the most famous of all Marine Corps symbols. It became part of the corps in 1868.

The Eagle, Globe, and Anchor emblem is made up of a globe that shows the **Western Hemisphere**, a ship's anchor, and a bald eagle. Over the years, the emblem came to represent Marine Corps service in the air, on land, and at sea. Upon completing **basic training**, marines are presented the emblem by their drill instructor.

Battle Colors

The official Marine Corps battle colors are kept at the marine **barracks** in Washington, D.C. The battle colors consist of 50 streamers representing everything from Marine Corps awards to the battles in which marines have fought, from the Revolutionary War to the present.

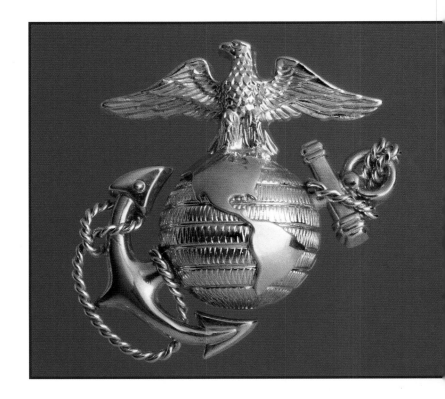

This is the Eagle, Globe, and Anchor Marine Corps emblem.

The Marine Corps seal

In 1954, President Dwight Eisenhower approved the design of an official Marine Corps seal. The seal was made up of the Eagle, Globe, and Anchor emblem, but the bald eagle replaced the crested eagle. The eagle holds in its beak a scroll on which the Marine Corps motto, *Semper fidelis,* is written.

The first Marine Corps flags date back to the Revolutionary War. In 1925, scarlet and gold were named the official Marine Corps colors. However, they were not added to the Marine Corps flag until 1939.

This Marine Corps officer is in his blue dress uniform with the sword. Note the bloodstripe on his pants.

The Bloodstripe
The red stripe found on the leg of a blue marine uniform is called a "bloodstripe." It symbolizes all the blood shed across the centuries by marines in battle.

The Marine Corps Band

The United States Marine Corps Band was started by an act of Congress in 1798. Its purpose is to play at functions in which the United States president or Marine Corps Commandant are present.

The band first played in the White House, before the building was completed. The White House was still under construction when President John Adams asked that the band play there on New Year's Day 1801.

Most members of the Marine Corps Band are graduates of the top music schools. More than half of them have earned advanced college degrees in music. They audition for the band just as if they are trying out for a famous symphony orchestra. They join the Marine Corps just to perform in the band.

Know It

The Marine Corps Band is the oldest professional group of musicians in the United States. It has played at every presidential inauguration since Thomas Jefferson's in 1801.

The Marine Corps marches during a victory parade in New York City after Operation Desert Storm in 1991.

The March King

John Philip Sousa is the most famous of all Marine Corps Band directors. He served as band director from 1880 to 1892. Under his leadership, the band became a world-class, internationally famous orchestra. The band then began traveling across the United States to present concerts. It also became one of the first musical groups to record a performance.

Sousa also was a composer. His military marches, which include "The Stars and Stripes Forever" and "The Washington Post," earned him the nickname the March King.

Today, the Marine Corps Band is very different from Sousa's time. Its performances are recorded on compact discs, and it offers concerts in many countries throughout the world.

John Philip Sousa

"President's Own"

The United States Marine Corps Band is known as the "President's Own." President Thomas Jefferson, who loved music and understood the importance of the band and its relationship to the presidency, gave the band this nickname.

Marines and Women

Opha Mae Johnson became the first of 305 women to enter the Marine Corps Reserve during World War I (1914–1918). At that time, women worked only in offices or in recruiting stations. This let the men, who would have done these jobs, fight in France. During World War II (1939–1945), women did more jobs. Some were still office workers, but many others were mechanics, mapmakers, and radio operators.

Even though women are not able to engage the enemy in direct **combat,** they are allowed to take part in martial arts training programs.

Keeping a Secret

Lucy Brewer grew up on a farm in Massachusetts. She arrived in Boston during the War of 1812. Dressed as a man, she joined the Marine Corps. Brewer was on hand during some of the war's most violent sea battles. No one discovered her secret. She revealed it only when she wrote a book about her life.

The Women's Reserve

The Marine Corps Women's Reserve was established in 1943, during World War II. It became a branch of the regular Marine Corps in 1948. Its original purpose was to place women in noncombat positions. This allowed men to be available for combat service.

Women became full-fledged marines in 1948. It was not until the 1970s, however, that women began receiving advanced technical training. In the mid-1970s, they were allowed to apply for all Marine Corps jobs, except for those that involved direct combat with the enemy.

Brigadier General
Margaret A. Brewer

Women as Officers

In 1978, Margaret A. Brewer became the Marine Corps' first **general officer.** She earned the rank of brigadier general. In 1992, Carol A. Mutter became the first woman to command a Marine **Fleet Force.** Two years later, Brigadier General Mutter became the marine's first woman major general. In 1993, Sarah Deal was the first woman marine to qualify for naval aviation training.

Lieutenant General
Carol A. Mutter

33

Marines and African Americans

African Americans served with the Continental Marines during the Revolutionary War (1775–1783). They were freemen. Isaac Walker was the first African-American Continental Marine. From then on, African Americans could not be marines until World War II (1939–1945).

After the United States entered the war in 1941, President Franklin D. Roosevelt signed an order allowing people of all races to be recruited into the armed forces. In 1942, African Americans were recruited into the Marine Corps. The Montford Point Marines was the first African-American marines **unit**. They trained at Montford Point Camp in New River, North Carolina. Only African-American Marine Corps **recruits** trained at Montford Point.

Even though they now were marines, African Americans still served in units that were separated from white soldiers. White officers commanded them.

First African-American Recruits

The first African-American recruits at Montford Point ranged in age from 17 to 29. Howard P. Petty of Charlotte, North Carolina, was the first of 20,000 recruits to arrive in the camp during the war.

Montford Point Marines run an obstacle course.

African-American marines take a rest during the battle for Tarawa in World War II.

Service in World War II

During World War II, Montford Point graduates served as ammunition handlers, truck drivers, and **stevedores** (loading and unloading ships). They were not allowed to have direct contact with the enemy in **combat**. They did, however, prove themselves by serving bravely in battles on the islands of Okinawa, Iwo Jima, and Peleliu in the Pacific Ocean.

Three Montford Point Marines had distinguished military careers. Edgar R. Huff was the first African-American sergeant major and spent 30 years in the Marine Corps. Gilbert "Hashmark" Johnson was one of the first African-American drill instructors. In 1945, Frederick C. Branch was the first African-American Marine Corps officer. He **retired** as a captain.

Know It

African-American marines training at Montford Point were kept apart from white marines. They only were able to enter Camp Lejeune, the neighboring Marine Corps base, if a white marine accompanied them.

Sergeant Major Edgar R. Huff (left) and Sergeant Major Gilbert "Hashmark" Johnson (right)

35

Equal status achieved

After World War II, the Marine Corps slowly began to integrate. Civil rights groups were demanding equal treatment for all people, including those in the military.

In 1948 President Harry S. Truman signed an order that officially granted equal treatment and opportunity for African Americans in the military. By 1949, Montford Point no longer was needed as a training camp for African Americans.

Almost 15,000 African-American marines finally served in **combat** during the Korean War (1950–1953). Second Lieutenant Frank E. Petersen Jr. was the first black Marine Corps pilot. He flew 64 combat missions and earned several medals.

Marines rest after a three-day battle with North Vietnamese troops in 1967.

In 1968, during the Vietnam War, Petersen was the first African American to command a fighter **squadron** in the United States Marine Corps or Navy. He also flew several hundred combat missions.

Frank E. Petersen had enlisted in the marines at age eighteen in 1950. He had a long military career and became the first African-American three-star general. When he **retired** in 1988, Petersen was a commanding general at the marine base in Quantico, Virginia.

Lieutenant General Frank E. Petersen Jr. grew up in Topeka, Kansas, just 10 miles (16 kilometers) from an army airfield used for World War II bombers.

Medal of Honor Winners

Five African Americans—James Anderson Jr., Oscar P. Austin, Ralph H. Johnson, Robert H. Jenkins Jr., and Rodney M. Davis—have been awarded the Medal of Honor. All served during the Vietnam War. All were honored posthumously (after they died in combat).

From left to right:
Private First Class James Anderson Jr., Private First Class Ralph H. Johnson, Private First Class Robert H. Jenkins Jr.

Medal of Honor

The Medal of Honor is the highest honor for bravery that can be awarded a person in the military. To earn the medal, a marine (or any member of the military) must risk his or her life during a military action. The feat must be exceptional. It must clearly demonstrate the soldier's courage beyond the call of duty. At least two eyewitnesses must testify that the feat occurred.

Know It

Because the Medal of Honor is granted "in the name of the Congress of the United States," it is often referred to as the Congressional Medal of Honor.

The Ceremony

In 1905, President Theodore Roosevelt signed an executive order in which he instructed that Medal of Honor award ceremonies always will be "formal and impressive." If possible, the honoree will be ordered to Washington, D.C. The president, in his role as commander in chief of the armed forces, or a representative of the president, will make the presentation.

The Congressional Medal of Honor

The Medal of Honor was first handed out during the Civil War (1861–1865). Corporal John F. Mackie was the first Marine Corps Medal of Honor recipient. He earned the award for his heroic actions while serving on board the USS *Galena*, a Union warship. Mackie was personally awarded the medal by President Abraham Lincoln.

Two marines—Major General Smedley D. Butler and Sergeant Major Daniel Daly—earned two Medals of Honor, on two separate occasions. Butler won his medals in 1915 for his heroism while serving as a marine in Mexico and Haiti. Daly earned his two for his actions in China in 1900 and Haiti in 1915.

Major General Alexander A. Vandergrift presents the Medal of Honor to Marine Sergeant Mitchell Paige at a 1943 ceremony in Australia. Paige had continued alone to direct machine-gun fire at Japanese troops after the rest of his **unit** was either killed or wounded. Moving from gun to gun, he fought until reinforcements arrived. Then he led a bayonet charge, driving the enemy back and preventing a break in the American lines.

Marine Corps War Memorial

The Marine Corps War Memorial is located in Washington, D.C. It honors the heroism of all United States Marines and especially their courage during one of the bloodiest battles of World War II.

That battle took place in 1945 on Iwo Jima, a Pacific Ocean island. The Japanese, one of the enemies the United States was fighting, controlled Iwo Jima. The island was between Japan and an airfield that U.S. bombers were using. It was important that Iwo Jima be taken from the enemy. The island would provide a place for damaged planes to land without having to fly all the way back to the airfield. To do this, 80,000 marines invaded the island and a fierce battle resulted. Almost 6,000 marines died and an additional 19,000 were wounded in the capture of Iwo Jima.

A Most Honored Platoon

For their valor on Iwo Jima, the 3rd **platoon** of E company, 2nd **battalion,** 28th Marine Regiment, 5th Marine Division became the most honored **unit** in marine history. Its members earned one Medal of Honor, one Silver Star, two Navy Crosses, seven Bronze Stars, and seventeen Purple Hearts.

Marines crawl up a slope on Iwo Jima toward Mount Surabachi in February 1945.

This is Joe Rosenthal's famous photo of the flag raising on Iwo Jima.

Raising the flag

One of the most dramatic moments during the battle for Iwo Jima was the raising of the American flag atop Mount Surabachi. Five marines—Michael Strank, Harlon H. Block, Franklin R. Sousley, Rene Gagnon, and Ira Hayes—and one navy hospital corpsman, John H. Bradley, together set up the flag. Joe Rosenthal, a news photographer, snapped a picture of the flag raising. Strank, Block, and Sousley were later killed in battle.

Rosenthal's photo served as a model for the Marine Corps War Memorial. The memorial is a 32-foot (almost 10-meters) high sculpture. President Dwight D. Eisenhower dedicated the war memorial on November 10, 1954. It is located near the northern end of Arlington National Cemetery.

Know It

The various flags raised on Mount Surabachi were rescued and preserved. They are on display at the Marine Corps Historical Center, located in the navy yard in Washington, D.C.

The Marine Corps War Memorial is in Washington, D.C.

Marine Corps Customs and Legends

Customs

Since the Marine Corps was established on November 10, 1775, that date was named as the corps' official birthday in 1921. At a Marine Corps birthday party, the oldest marine on hand receives the first piece of birthday cake. The youngest receives the second.

Chief Warrant Officer Eduardo A. Foster (center), the oldest marine present, watches Lance Corporal Adam E. Jurewich, the youngest marine, eat a piece of birthday cake at the Marine Corps birthday celebration in Albany, Georgia, in 2002.

The youngest marines are also part of another custom. When getting on a small boat or entering a car, younger marines go first and use the seats or the space at the front. The older, more senior marines enter last and are the first to leave.

Talk Like a Marine

The marines have their own special way of describing things. Most of these terms are from the days when marines were mostly on ships. Today, even marines based on land use these terms:

head (bathroom)
rack (bunk bed)
topside (upstairs)
down below (downstairs)

deck (floor)
bulkhead (wall)
overhead (ceiling)
porthole (window)

The leather collar shown here was covered by a dress shirt and worn by an 18th-century marine.

Traditions

Between the 1790s and 1870s, marines wore leather collars around their necks. It was supposed to make the collars stand straighter and was part of the full-dress uniform. But one general said it made the wearers appear "like geese looking for rain." It was last used in 1872. But the nickname "leatherneck" is still used for marines today.

They also are called "devil dogs." After the marines battled the Germans in the Belleau Wood during World War I (1914–1918), the Germans used the word *teufelhunden* to describe the marines. *Teufelhunden* is German for "fierce fighting dogs of legendary origin" or, simply translated, "devil dogs."

Legend of buried treasure

It is said that during the War of 1812 (1812–1815), two marine sergeants buried a chest filled with money somewhere in marine headquarters as the British army neared Washington, D.C. Both marines soon were killed. The location of the treasure died with them.

Know It

Ever since the last New Year's Day of the Civil War (1861–1865), the Marine Corps Band has performed at the home of the Marine Corps Commandant on the morning of January 1. After the music stops, band members are rewarded with breakfast and hot buttered rum.

The Marines' Hymn

The Marines' Hymn has been performed around the world. It is one of the world's most famous military songs. The story goes that a soldier from the Mexican War (1846–1848) wrote the first verse of the hymn. He set the words to a Mexican folk tune. The hymn originally began, "From the shores of Tripoli to the halls of Montezuma" but the phrases were later switched. The hymn first became popular during the Civil War (1861–1865).

The phrase "from the halls of Montezuma" refers to Marine Corps activities during the Mexican War. "To the shores of Tripoli" refers to the 1805 capture by marines of Arab fighters at the port of Derna, in Tripoli, North Africa, during the Tripolitan War (1801–1805).

Know It

Upon the singing or playing of the Marines' Hymn, all marines must rise and remain standing until its completion.

The Marine Corps Band marched at the St. Louis World's Fair in 1904.

The Marine Corps Band often plays at the White House.

The hymn's tune is from a French comic opera that was first presented in Paris in 1859. Over the years, different verses have been added. They have also been changed to match events in different wars. The Marine Corps Commandant authorized the "official" version in 1929.

During World War II (1939–1945), the first marine aviators played a large part in fighting for their country. To honor them, the Marines' Hymn line "On the land as on the sea" was changed to "In the air, on land and sea."

The Hymn

Here is the most popular official verse of the Marines' Hymn:

"From the Halls of Montezuma
to the Shores of Tripoli,
We fight our country's battles
In the air, on land and sea.
First to fight for right and freedom,
And to keep our honor clean,
We are proud to claim the title
of United States Marine."

Glossary

active duty workds full time in the military

amphibious assault vehicle vehicle that operates both on land and water

artillery gun or missile that is mounted on a vehicle

barracks building where new members of the armed forces live during basic training, while they learn military behavior, duties, and combat skills

battalion two or more military units made up of soldiers who fight on land

boot camp camp where new members of the military are trained

combat active fighting

communications means of exchanging information; for example, by radio, telephone, or e-mail

communist belonging to a system in which all goods and property are to be shared

Continental Congress two lawmaking congresses that were held during and after the Revolutionary War

data information

embassies offices in countries abroad where diplomats work, usually headed by an ambassador

emblem symbol

enlistment period amount of time that a person has agreed to serve in an armed force

fixed-wing aircraft airplane whose wings are tightly attached to its body

fleet force major group of warships and aircraft in the United States military

general officer officer whose rank is above that of colonel

gun turrets structures, located in forts or on ships, where guns are mounted

infantry military branch whose members fight on foot

infrared invisible rays of light

light-armored vehicle car that has eight-wheels, is armed with cannons, and is used for reconnaissance purposes

Marine Expeditionary Forces three major marine combat organizations outside the United States

marksmanship ability to hit a target every time

mortar cannon that fires shells at high angles

navigator person who keeps a moving vehicle such as an airplane or helicopter on its proper course

navy yard waterside site where ships are built and repaired

platoon group of 16 to 44 soldiers

radar device used for detecting and locating aircraft

reconnaissance search to obtain military information from or about the enemy

recruit new members of the armed forces

respiratory system organs that allow people to breathe including the lungs and the circulatory and nervous systems connected to them

retired no longer working

rotary-wing aircraft helicopter

scholarship gift of money, usually for education

sharpshooter person who can hit a target accurately

squadron military group of at least four people

state-of-the-art latest development in a technology or method

stevedores persons who load and unload cargo from ships

units parts of military organizations that make up a whole

Western Hemisphere continents of North and South America plus nearby islands and water

More Books to Read

Aaseng, Nathan. *The Marine Corps in Action.* Berkeley Heights, N.J.: Enslow Publishing, 2001.

Abramovitz, Melissa. *The U.S. Marine Corps at War.* Mankato, Minn.: Capstone Press, 2002.

Kennedy, Robert C. *Life in the Marines.* Danbury, Conn.: Children's Press, 2000.

Index